STENCILING
BASICS

2 Tools

6 Techniques

    6 Surface Preparation

    7 Loading a Stencil Brush

    8 How to Stencil

    9 Masking Stencil Areas

    10 Creating Your Own Stencil

    12 Aligning Letters

    13 Cleaning Stencils

    13 Cleaning Tools

    13 Covering Mistakes

14 Projects

    14 "Market" Burlap Canvas

    16 Peony Blanket Chest

    18 Flower Pots

    20 Medallion Lampshade

    22 "LOVE" Letters

    24 Magnetic Memo Board

    26 Framed Monograms

    28 Jute Rug

    30 Make Your Own State Plaque

For more project ideas and inspiration, visit www.plaidonline.com

D1214656

LEISURE ARTS, INC. • Maumelle, Arkansas

TOOLS

FolkArt® Mylar Laser Cut Single Layer Stencils

- Great for everyday craft projects, large or small
- Can be cleaned and reused many times

FolkArt® Mylar Laser Cut 3 Sheet Layering Stencils

- Sized and scaled specifically for home decor projects
- Each pack contains 3 pieces: Silhouette, Pattern, and Mask
- Stencil can be layered many ways to create a variety of effects
- Durable and reusable

FolkArt® Peel & Stick Painting Stencils

- Low-tack adhesive adheres firmly to project surface, preventing paint run-unders
- Flexible material allows stenciling on curved surfaces
- Sticks to any non-porous surface; repositionable up to 20 times
- Also available as blanks to create your own stencil

FolkArt® Sponges

- Natural sea sponges; no two exactly alike
- Loose, open cells give stenciling a different look
- Wet the sponge, wrap in a paper towel, and squeeze out the excess moisture before loading with paint

FolkArt® Stencil Brushes

- High-quality, white bristle brushes
- Solid wood handles
- Seamless aluminium ferrules
- Firm, yet flexible bristles; will spring back to the original shape
- Available in four sizes: $1/4$", $3/8$", $1/2$", and $5/8$"

FolkArt® Stencil Roller

- Foam roller
- Great for stenciling large areas, such as floors or walls
- Can also be used to basecoat large areas quickly

FolkArt® Spouncers

- Circular foam sponge attached to a wooden handle
- Available in three sizes: $3/4$", $1\,1/4$", and $1\,3/4$"
- The stencil design will appear more opaque when painted with a spouncer
- Creates perfect circles

FolkArt® Daubers

- Great little tool: dense foam attached at one end
- Two sizes: $1/4$" and $5/8$"
- Soft, even application of paint
- Creates perfect polka dots

FolkArt® Multi-Surface Acrylic Paint

- Complete coverage for almost every surface
- For indoor and outdoor projects; dishwasher safe
- Smooth, creamy consistency that dries to a satin finish

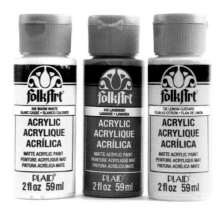

FolkArt® Acrylic Paint

- All-purpose, artist-quality acrylics; perfect for stenciling
- Smooth, creamy consistency that dries to a matte finish
- Highly pigmented for superior coverage

FolkArt® Outdoor Acrylic Paint

- Superior UV protection and weather-resistance
- Self-sealing—no primers, sealers, or varnishes needed
- Dries to an opaque, gloss finish

FolkArt® Home Decor Chalk

- Ultra matte chalk finish
- No sanding or priming needed
- Perfect for layering and distressing

Basic Tools

foam plates • paper towels • scissors • craft knife • chalkboard chalk • pencil • tape measure • ruler • brush basin • assortment of bristle and foam stencil brushes in various sizes • stencil tape or stencil adhesive • tack cloth • sandpaper • rubbing alcohol

TECHNIQUES

SURFACE PREPARATION

When stenciling, it is very important to properly prepare your surface. If you take the time to create something, you will want to make sure it will endure the test of time! Let's explore the variety of surfaces which can be stenciled and how to prepare them.

Wood: If your wood surface is rough, it should first be sanded with a fine-grit to medium-grit sandpaper. After sanding, remove the sanding dust with either a damp paper towel or a tack cloth. Once smooth and clean, the wood surface can then be painted a basecoat color. When dry, if the basecoat has raised the grain of the wood, sand smooth using fine-grit sandpaper, then reapply the base color. Allow to thoroughly dry before stenciling.

Walls: Remove dirt, dust, or grease marks by cleaning the wall. If painting the wall with a fresh coat of paint, be sure to use either latex or an oil-base paint in a flat, eggshell, or satin finish which will allow FolkArt Acrylic paints and FolkArt Home Decor Chalk to adhere well. Allow freshly painted walls to dry thoroughly before stenciling.

Fabric: Denims, cottons, poly/blends, closely woven fabrics, and home decor textiles are best for stenciling. All fabrics should be washed in warm soapy water to remove dirt as well as manufacturer's sizing. Most denim fabrics should be washed multiple times in hot water to thoroughly remove the sizing. Allow to dry and iron to remove wrinkles. Do not use fabric softeners, dryer sheets, or spray starch as this may prevent the paints from adhering properly to the fabric.

Terra Cotta: To prepare new terra cotta for stenciling, wipe the surface clean with a damp cloth or paper towel to remove dirt or dust. If desired, apply a basecoat or two of FolkArt Acrylic paint to color the terra cotta prior to stenciling. Spray the interior of the flower pot with FolkArt Clear Acrylic Spray Sealer prior to use. This prevents excess moisture from seeping through the pot and blistering the exterior painted finish.

Papier-Mâché: Simply wipe the surface with a damp cloth or paper towel. Once clean, apply one to two coats of FolkArt Acrylic paint to add a base of color to your stenciling surface.

Glass/Ceramics: Glass and ceramic surfaces should be thoroughly cleaned in warm soapy water and rinsed well to remove any dirt, dust, grease or oils from your hands. Allow to dry. Moisten a paper towel with rubbing alcohol, then wipe over the cleaned glass surface to remove any remaining grease or soap residue.

Canvas: Wipe primed canvas clean with a dampened cloth to remove dust. If unprimed, apply a coat or two of gesso, allowing the first application to thoroughly dry before applying the second.

Tin/Metal: Wash with warm soapy water; allow to dry. Wipe the metal surface with a white vinegar dampened cloth or paper towel and allow to dry.

LOADING A STENCIL BRUSH

Most stenciling is completed using a "dry brush" technique where you load paint onto your brush evenly across the entire surface then remove or "off-load" paint creating a dry brush with color. If you were to stencil immediately after loading the brush, your stenciled design will be heavy and the paint may bleed under the stencil.

Begin by dipping the bristle end of your dry stencil brush into a small puddle of paint. Tap the bristles up and down on a clean area to ensure all bristles are loaded with paint *(Photo 1)*.

Off-load the excess paint by pressing the paint-loaded bristles into a paper towel to remove most of the paint *(Photo 2)*.

HOW TO STENCIL

There are two main techniques used: The Circular Motion and The Stippling Motion.

The Circular Motion: Many stenciling purists prefer the "circular motion" technique where the stencil brush is held straight up at a 90 degree angle to the surface *(Photo 3)*. The brush is then moved lightly in a circular motion clockwise and then counter-clockwise around the stencil design beginning at the center of the stencil and working toward the stencil outer edges *(Photo 4)*.

The Stippling Motion: Another technique often used when stenciling with sponges, daubers, and spouncers, is a stippling or dabbing up and down motion. Simply pounce or dab your stencil tool straight up and down over the stencil *(Photo 5)*. Stencil brushes may also be used for this technique.

MASKING STENCIL AREAS

It is easy to create a multi-colored stencil design when using single layer or multi-layer stencils. Simply mask or tape over sections of the stencil one color at a time. For example, when stenciling a medallion design with many sections, place stencil tape over all the areas not stenciled the same color *(Photo 6, which shows Lime Green being stenciled)*; then remove the stencil tape and reapply to mask any sections that are not to be stenciled with the next color.

CREATING YOUR OWN STENCIL

Although there are a variety of stencil designs available today, you may want to create your own personal stencil. Follow either one of these two methods and you will successfully create your own stencil!

Stencil Burning: Choose your line art drawing to make into a stencil. Position the drawing on your work surface. Lay a sheet of glass (with taped edges) over the drawing. Next, place a sheet of mylar stencil material over the glass pane and secure with stencil tape. Allow your stencil burner to heat up. "Draw" over the pattern lines which can be seen through both the mylar and pane of glass *(Photo 7)*.

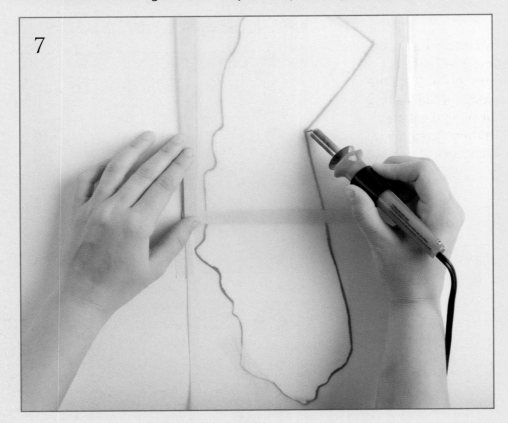

7

Tip: IT IS ALWAYS EASIER TO PULL THE STENCIL BURNER OR CRAFT KNIFE TOWARD YOURSELF, SO TURN YOUR WORK OFTEN.

Stencil Cutting: A stencil design can also be cut from mylar using a craft knife with a sharp blade. Layer the pattern, glass, and mylar as described in the Stencil Burning instructions and then cut along the pattern lines *(Photo 8)*.

Or, you can trace the pattern onto the mylar using a fine-point permanent ink marker, then cut along the marker lines *(Photo 9)*.

A third method for cutting a stencil: tape the paper pattern to a self-adhesive stencil blank or mylar blank. Place the blank on glass or a self-healing cutting mat and slowly cut along the pattern lines *(Photo 10)*, cutting through both the paper pattern and stencil material.

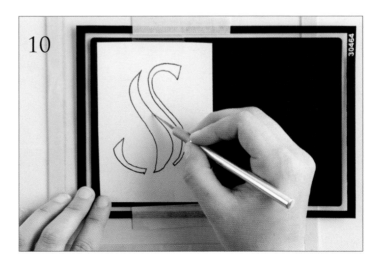

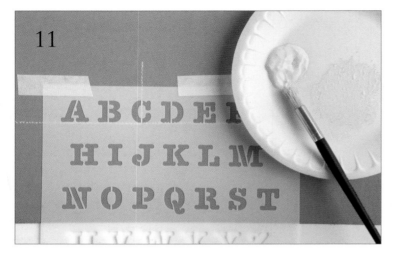

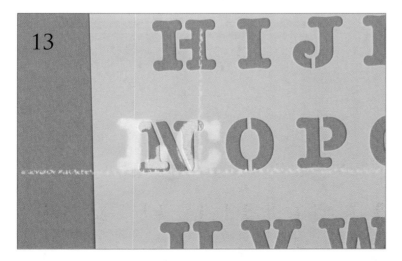

ALIGNING LETTERS

For perfect letter alignment when stenciling a word with an alphabet stencil, start off by drawing a baseline with chalkboard chalk. Draw a vertical chalk line at the center of the word. Always begin stenciling at the center letter.

For example, to stencil "Welcome," find the center of the area to be stenciled and draw your chalk guidelines. Next position the "C" in that center spot *(Photo 11)* and stencil "C".

Working from that center outwards, stencil each letter to the left and right, one at a time, *(Photos 12 and 13)*, allowing each stenciled letter to dry first before laying the stencil over the previous letter(s).

CLEANING STENCILS

To prolong the life of your mylar stencils be sure to clean them after each use or often when stenciling a large project such as a wall. To clean them when using water-base paints, rinse well under running water. If paint has dried on the stencil, wipe over the dried paint with a rubbing alcohol dampened paper towel. If there are several layers of paint, immerse the stencil in a bath of rubbing alcohol which will cut through the layers of built up paint. Then rinse in warm water.

CLEANING TOOLS

It is essential to clean the remaining paint from your stencil tools immediately after each use. Never ruin a stenciling tool by allowing paint to dry on the tool. To clean your stencil brushes, sponges, daubers, spouncers, and rollers, immediately rinse them in cool water and then lather with mild soap. Rinse until all paint has been removed.

COVERING MISTAKES

When stenciling, an occasional paint mistake can happen. If caught immediately, quickly clean up the excess paint with a moist paper towel. Once dried, a little rubbing alcohol on a paper towel may remove the paint smudge. If this does not help, repaint over the paint smudge using the base color of the project. Always check and if necessary, clean the back of the stencil where paint may have smudged.

"MARKET" burlap canvas

TECHNIQUE: Stenciling with a Stencil Brush

SHOPPING LIST

- [ ] 11" x 14" Unfinished wood frame with wide molding
- [ ] 11" x 14" Stretched burlap canvas
- [ ] FolkArt® 2-piece Vintage Crate Laser Stencil
- [ ] FolkArt® Multi-Surface Acrylic Paint (Licorice)
- [ ] FolkArt® Home Decor Chalk (Nantucket Blue, White Adirondack)
- [ ] FolkArt® 3/8" Stencil Brush
- [ ] FolkArt® Home Decor Chalk Brush
- [ ] FolkArt® Home Decor Layering Block
- [ ] FolkArt® Stencil Tape
- [ ] Basic tools

Be sure to read & familiarize yourself with the information on pages 2-13 before beginning your project.

Tip: PLAN YOUR PROJECT TO USE A VARIETY OF DESIGN ELEMENTS IN DIFFERENT WAYS.

To make the Framed Canvas:

1. Clean the frame with window cleaner to remove any dirt or dust particles. Basecoat the entire frame with White Adirondack; allow to dry.

2. Decide on the arrangement of the phrases and numbers on the burlap canvas. Any component of the stencil can be used as a whole or in part. Use the chalkboard chalk to lightly mark where each design element will be. Tape the stencil to the canvas.

3. Squeeze a small amount of Licorice onto a foam plate. Load the stencil brush by dipping into the paint puddle. Swirl brush on a paper towel to off-load most of the paint creating a "dry brush."

4. Using a small circular motion, stencil each design element (one at a time) with Licorice. Allow to dry.

5. Pour some Nantucket Blue paint onto a foam plate. Dip the Layering Block into the paint and lightly blot on a clean area of the plate. Drag the block over the painted frame, just skimming the surface creating a distressed look. Allow to dry.

6. Lightly drag the Layering Block (with Nantucket Blue) over the canvas edges; allow to dry. Insert the canvas into the frame.

PEONY
blanket chest

SHOPPING LIST

- ☐ Wood storage chest (ours is 31" x 16" x 18")
- ☐ FolkArt® Peony Laser Cut Wall Stencil
- ☐ FolkArt® Paisley Painting Stencil
- ☐ FolkArt® Home Decor Chalk (Castle, Sheepskin, Yellow Crochet)
- ☐ FolkArt® Home Decor Wide Chalk Brush
- ☐ FolkArt® ⁵/₈" Stencil Brush
- ☐ FolkArt® Stencil Tape
- ☐ FolkArt® Basecoating Brush Set
- ☐ Basic tools

Be sure to read & familiarize yourself with the information on pages 2-13 before beginning your project.

To make the Chest:

1. Clean the chest with window cleaner to remove any dirt or dust particles. Basecoat the chest lid with Castle. Basecoat the chest base with Sheepskin. Allow to dry.

2. Tape the Paisley stencil to the chest base. Using a small circular motion, stencil the paisley design randomly around the entire base with Yellow Crochet.

3. Tape the Peony stencil to the chest base right under the lid with about ³/₄ of the flower on the base. Stencil with Castle.

4. Tape the Peony stencil to the lid right above the partial flower with the remaining ¹/₄ of the flower on the lid. Stencil with Sheepskin. Referring to the photo for placement, stencil two more partial flowers on the lid.

5. Paint the trim on the chest bottom Castle and Yellow Crochet as shown.

Tip: CREATE A STENCILED RANDOM PATTERN BY ROTATING THE PAISLEY STENCIL FOR EACH REPEAT.

FLOWER pots

SHOPPING LIST

☐ Assorted dark color flower pots

☐ FolkArt® Borders Peel & Stick Painting Stencil

☐ FolkArt® Outdoor Acrylic Paint (Thicket, Wicker White)

☐ FolkArt® Daubers

☐ FolkArt® Clear Acrylic Spray Sealer

☐ Basic tools

Be sure to read & familiarize yourself with the information on pages 2-13 before beginning your project.

Tip: SPRAY TERRA COTTA POT INTERIORS WITH SEVERAL LIGHT COATS OF ACRYLIC SEALER BEFORE YOU BEGIN. THIS WILL PREVENT THE EXTERIOR PAINT FROM BLISTERING.

To make each Pot:

1. Referring to the photo for placement, position the Peel & Stick border stencil on the flower pot.

2. Squeeze a small amount of paint onto a foam plate. Load the dauber with paint by dipping into the paint puddle. Dab up and down on a clean spot on the plate to off-load the excess paint.

3. Stencil the border design by dabbing up and down, applying the paint through the stencil openings. Continue the dabbing up and down motion until the entire border has been painted. Lift and remove the stencil immediately after stenciling. Allow the paint to dry before realigning the Peel & Stick stencil and continuing to stencil the border.

4. Let paint dry for at least 12 hours before using outdoors.

MEDALLION
lampshade

SHOPPING LIST

- ☐ Lampshade (ours is a 14½" dia. x 12" h drum shade)
- ☐ FolkArt® Medallion Mask Laser Cut Stencil
- ☐ FolkArt® Multi-Surface Acrylic Paint (Aqua, Bright Green, Daffodil Yellow, Ink Spot, Lime Green)
- ☐ FolkArt® Home Decor Chalk (Parisian Grey)
- ☐ FolkArt® ⅝" Stencil Brush
- ☐ FolkArt® ¼" Stencil Brush (stenciling is easier if you have 1 brush for each color)
- ☐ FolkArt® Stencil Tape
- ☐ Basic tools

Be sure to read & familiarize yourself with the information on pages 2-13 before beginning your project.

Tip: WORKING ASSEMBLY-LINE STYLE, COMPLETE A COLOR ON THE LAMPSHADE BEFORE MOVING ON TO THE NEXT COLOR, RATHER THAN COMPLETING EACH MEDALLION.

To make the Lampshade:

1. Mark a very light pencil line horizontally around the lampshade's vertical center.

2. Center the medallion Silhouette layer of the stencil on the pencil mark; tape in place. Pour a small amount of Parisian Grey onto a foam plate. Load the ⅝" stencil brush by dipping into the paint puddle. Swirl brush on a paper towel to remove most of the paint creating a "dry brush."

3. Using a small circular motion, stencil the medallion shape onto the lampshade with a base of Parisian Grey. Remove the stencil immediately. Reposition the Silhouette layer to the left and right of the origianal medallion as shown in the photo. Tape in place and repeat the stenciling process around the lamp. Continue building the overall pattern by offsetting partial medallions at the top and bottom of the shade. Allow to dry.

4. Tape off or mask areas of the Pattern layer stencil that will not be painted with Ink Spot. Position the stencil over the basecoated silhouette pattern and tape in place. Squeeze a small amount of Ink Spot onto a foam plate. Load the stencil brush with Ink Spot and off-load excess onto a paper towel. Using a pouncing motion, apply Ink Spot to the stencil areas. Remove the stencil immediately. Continue around the entire lampshade. Allow the paint to dry.

5. Repeat Step 4, taping off all open areas that will not be painted Lime Green. Continue painting in this manner with Aqua, Bright Green, and Daffodil Yellow.

"LOVE" letters

TECHNIQUE: Stenciling with a Sea Sponge

SHOPPING LIST

- ☐ Papier-mâché letters to spell "LOVE" (ours are 11½" high)
- ☐ FolkArt® Damask Painting Stencil
- ☐ FolkArt® Moroccan Tile Painting Stencil
- ☐ FolkArt® Acrylic Paint (Wicker White)
- ☐ FolkArt® Sponge Value Pack
- ☐ FolkArt® Stencil Tape
- ☐ Basic tools

Be sure to read & familiarize yourself with the information on pages 2-13 before beginning your project.

To make each Letter:

1. Prepare the sea sponge by wetting with water and then wrapping it with a paper towel and squeezing to remove the excess moisture.

2. Decide on the placement of the stencil and tape in place on a letter.

3. Squeeze a small amount of paint onto a foam plate. Load the sponge with paint by dipping into the paint puddle. Dab up and down on a clean paper towel, blotting to remove the excess paint.

4. Begin stenciling by dabbing up and down, applying the paint through the stencil openings. Continue the dabbing up and down motion until the entire stencil design has been painted. Reposition the stencil as necessary to completely cover the letter surfaces.

Tip: SEA SPONGES CAN BE CUT INTO SMALLER SIZES TO ALLOW FOR EASIER PAINT APPLICATION.

MAGNETIC
memo board

SHOPPING LIST

- [ ] Large metal tray (ours is 11³/₄" x 16")
- [ ] FolkArt® Arrow Pattern Painting Stencil
- [ ] FolkArt® Multi-Surface Acrylic Paint (Metallic 14K Gold, Wicker White)
- [ ] FolkArt® 1³/₄" Spouncer
- [ ] FolkArt® ¹/₄" Stencil Brush
- [ ] FolkArt® Basecoating Brush Set
- [ ] FolkArt® Stencil Tape
- [ ] FolkArt® Clear Acrylic Spray Sealer
- [ ] 1¹/₄ yards of 2" wide wire-edged ribbon
- [ ] Basic tools

Be sure to read & familiarize yourself with the information on pages 2-13 before beginning your project.

To make the Memo Board:

1. Wash the tray with warm soapy water; rinse and allow to dry. Wipe the tray with a white vinegar dampened cloth; allow to dry.

2. Using the 1³/₄" spouncer, apply the Metallic 14K Gold paint to the tray. Allow to dry. Apply a second coat of paint with the basecoating brush. You may need to add several more coats to completely cover the tray. Allow each coat of paint to dry before applying the next coat.

3. Tape the Arrow Pattern stencil to the tray. Using the stencil brush and a small circular motion, stencil the arrow pattern with Wicker White, repositioning the stencil as necessary to completely cover the tray.

4. Let paint dry for at least 12 hours before spraying with the acrylic sealer. For the hanger, cut the ribbon in half and thread the ribbons through a handle. Tie the ribbons in a bow.

Tip: TO REPEAT A STENCIL, POSITION THE STENCIL ON TOP OF THE LAST ROW OF WHAT WAS PREVIOUSLY STENCILED.

FRAMED
monograms

SHOPPING LIST

- ☐ 4" x 6" Wood frame with glass for each letter
- ☐ Computer printout of desired letter(s) in desired size (ours are about $3\frac{1}{2}$" high)
- ☐ FolkArt® Blank Peel & Stick Painting Stencil (one sheet for each letter)
- ☐ FolkArt® Folklore Peel & Stick Painting Stencil
- ☐ FolkArt® Multi-Surface Acrylic Paint (Licorice, Pearl Mandarin Satin, Patina)
- ☐ FolkArt® Home Decor Chalk (Rich Black, Yellow Crochet)
- ☐ FolkArt® Home Decor Chalk Brush
- ☐ FolkArt® Daubers
- ☐ FolkArt® Stencil Tape
- ☐ E6000® Industrial Strength Adhesive
- ☐ Glass pane or self-healing cutting mat (a bit larger than the letter)
- ☐ Basic tools

Be sure to read & familiarize yourself with the information on pages 2-13 before beginning your project.

To make each Monogram:

1. Remove the glass from the frame. Clean the frame with window cleaner to remove any dirt or dust particles. Use the chalk brush to basecoat the frame with Rich Black; allow to dry for 2 hours. Apply a coat of Yellow Crochet; allow to dry. Lightly sand the frame to allow some of the Rich Black to show through, creating a distressed look.

2. To make the stencil, tape the printout of the letter to the face of the adhesive stencil blank. Place on the glass pane or cutting mat and use the craft knife to cut out the letter stencil, cutting through the paper and the stencil blank.

3. Clean the frame glass with window cleaner. Place the letter stencil on the glass and using the dauber and a pouncing motion, stencil the letter with Licorice. Remove the stencil and allow to dry.

4. Center the flower border stencil below the letter and stencil the flowers with Patina and Pearl Mandarin. Remove the stencil and allow to dry.

5. Use E6000 to adhere the glass to the frame.

Tip: POSITION THE CENTER OF THE STENCIL LETTER A LITTLE HIGHER THAN THE CENTER OF THE GLASS PANE TO ALLOW FOR THE STENCILED FLOWER BORDER.

JUTE rug

TECHNIQUE: Stenciling with Tape

SHOPPING LIST

- ☐ Jute rug (ours is 20" x 30")
- ☐ FolkArt® Multi-Surface Acrylic Paint (Deep Blue Ocean, Ink Spot, Patina)
- ☐ FolkArt® ⅝" Stencil Brush (stenciling is easier if you have one brush for each color)
- ☐ FolkArt® Stencil Tape
- ☐ Basic tools

Be sure to read & familiarize yourself with the information on pages 2-13 before beginning your project.

Tip: TO CREATE WIDER STRIPES, APPLY TWO PIECES OF TAPE SIDE BY SIDE, FIRMLY PRESSING THE EDGES DOWN.

To make the Rug:

1. Lay rug on a flat surface. Use stencil tape to tape off the rug as shown in **Fig. 1**. Be sure to press the tape down as securely as possible, especially along the edges.

Fig. 1

2. Squeeze a paint color onto a foam plate. Load stencil brush by dipping into the paint puddle; do **not** dab brush or blot off any paint.

3. Beginning at the center of the area to be stenciled and working toward the tape, pounce the paint onto the rug. Pick up more paint on the brush as needed. Repeat with each paint color, following the photo for color placement. Do not remove the tape.

4. After the paint has completely dried, remove the tape.